T0145038

DARLENE BEAZER-PARKER

Copyright © 2020 Darlene Beazer-Parker.

All rights reserved. No part of this book may be used or reproduced by any means,
graphic, electronic, or mechanical, including photocopying, recording, taping or by
any information storage retrieval system without the written permission of the author
except in the case of brief quotations embodied in critical articles and reviews.

This book is a work of non-fiction. Unless otherwise noted, the author and the publisher
make no explicit guarantees as to the accuracy of the information contained in this book and
in some cases, names of people and places have been altered to protect their privacy.

Archway Publishing books may be ordered through booksellers or by contacting:

Archway Publishing
1663 Liberty Drive
Bloomington, IN 47403
www.archwaypublishing.com
1 (888) 242-5904

Because of the dynamic nature of the Internet, any web addresses or links contained in
this book may have changed since publication and may no longer be valid. The views
expressed in this work are solely those of the author and do not necessarily reflect the views
of the publisher, and the publisher hereby disclaims any responsibility for them.

Any people depicted in stock imagery provided by Getty Images are models,
and such images are being used for illustrative purposes only.
Certain stock imagery © Getty Images.

Waiting All Year photograph courtesy of Mohammid Walbrook.
Aerial photograph of Barbuda courtesy of George Wehner.

ISBN: 978-1-4808-8827-2 (sc)
ISBN: 978-1-4808-8828-9 (hc)
ISBN: 978-1-4808-8826-5 (e)

Print information available on the last page.

Archway Publishing rev. date: 6/2/2020

Acknowledgements

I give thanks for all the guardians of the Codrington Lagoon, for the elders who used the gifts of the sea sustainably and for the freedom we have as children of Barbuda to enjoy such a prized possession. Thanks to my family and especially my niece Zinzi, for her comments and reviews. Giving thanks to God always for the bounty and beauty of BARBUDA.

It's summer time, bright, blazing sun;
from the village, the children run

Down to the lagoon to swim and play;
where they are free, free all day.

Codrington lagoon is where
Barbudan children learn to swim.
Portsmouth is where the lessons begin.

Crawl on the sand, paddle, or wade;
some quietly watch from the shade.

Sometimes to get over the fear,
holding your sister's hand
will get you there,

When paddles and dives they can manage,
the head of wharf is a swimmer's challenge.

As your confidence develops
and swimming skills grow,
Ready, steady, set,

Go!

Jumping from the wharf or
the side of a moored boat
We share a bond as we bob and float.

Our style may be different
but, it doesn't matter

We all give a cheer as our
friends hit the water

Dive, back flip, belly flop,
summertime freedom we share

Hurry, take the last plunge,
the evening's draws near

By summer's end, we go to
Carty's wharf to explore

Planting mangrove seedlings at the end of the day, to preserve our lagoon for future children's play.

Summer days are here to stay,

Please don't ever go away!

Photo courtesy of Mohammid Walbrook

Photo courtesy of Mohammid Walbrook

THE END

Codrington Lagoon

A central feature of Barbuda is Codrington Lagoon which is a unique and highly vulnerable component the only site designated as wetlands of International Importance (Ramsar Site no. 1488), with a surface an area of 3,600 hectares (18km2 (12 km north to south and 4 km wide). The depths range from <0.5m to 4 m. From north to south it is the most significant element of Barbuda's coastal Zones. The lagoon serves as a habitat and nursery for a range of marine species, due to its protective and sheltered distinctiveness of extensive fringing mangroves and sea-grass beds. The lagoon also supports one of the world's largest colonies of Frigate birds (*Fregata magnificens*). The Frigate Bird Sanctuary was designated a National Park to conserve and protect this globally important sanctuary.

Today it has become a prized tourist attraction. The lagoon is used for several activities; Fishing (pots, lines, diving, and net fishing). Tourism (visits to the Bird Sanctuary, use of beaches on the west coast) Leisure and Recreation (harbor for small fishing vessels; bathing of domestic animals; occasional sailboat racing; parties and fund-raising events such as fish fries around the wharf area; water skiing, and other water sports. One of the main activities done in the lagoon is swimming. It has been said that all Barbudians have learned to swim in the lagoon. An additional activity is that each morning; around 5:00 a.m. older folks walk down to the lagoon for their early morning swim therapy, for whatever their ailment may be. Many have touted the healing properties of the waters of the lagoon.

The mangroves along the lagoon sustain the balance of the ecosystem of the oceans of the Caribbean and the world. Barbudans are passionate about protecting the lagoon and the life it sustains.

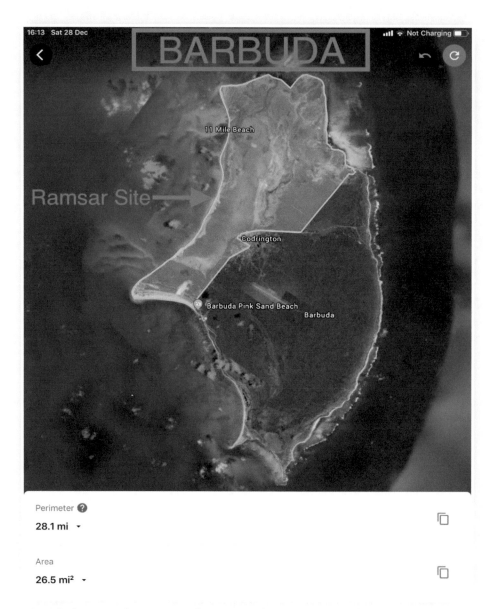

Aerial photograph courtesy of George Wehner

Summertime Fun

Its summer time, bright, blazing sun;
from the village, the children run
Down to the lagoon to swim and play;
where they are free, free all day.
Codrington lagoon is where Barbudan children learned to swim.
Portsmouth is where the lessons begin.
Crawl on the sand, paddle, or wade,
some quietly watch from the shade.
Sometimes to get over the fear,
holding your sister's hand will get you there,
When paddles and dives they can manage,
the head of wharf swimmer's challenge.
As your confidence develops and swimming skills grow,
Ready, steady, set, GO!
Jumping from the wharf or the side of a moored boat
We share a bond as we bob and float
Our style may be different but, it doesn't matter
We all give a cheer as our friends hit the water
Dive, back flip, belly flop, summertime freedom we share
Hurry, take the last plunge, the evening's draws near
By summer's end, we go to Carty's wharf to explore
Planting mangrove seedlings at the end of the day,
to preserve our lagoon for future children's play.
Summer days are here to stay,
Please don't ever go away!

Growing up in Barbuda, I could hardly wait for summer to spend all day at the lagoon. We swam, fished, cooked and played until the sun went down. As the day wore on, we could hear our parents call our names to come home.

Printed in the United States
By Bookmasters